Thank you!

Thank you for choosing our coloring book! This is not just a coloring book; created by two sisters with a shared passion for teaching children about Jesus, this book was lovingly designed to make learning about His love and teachings fun and engaging. We hope it brings joy to little hearts, sparks curiosity about God's Word, and helps families grow closer in faith. Your support means the world to us, and we pray this book blesses your family as much as creating it has blessed us.

Blessings,
Kylie Hoobler & Nina Pulliam

ADAM & EVE

Adam and Eve were the first people that God created. Adam was made from the ground, and Eve was created from Adam to be his partner. They lived in a beautiful garden, called Eden. God made them to help him take care of his creation. They disobeyed God, by listening to the sneaky serpent and eating from the Tree of Knowledge of Good and Evil. After that, they had to leave the garden. This story teaches us the difference between right and wrong and the consequences of our choices.

THINK ABOUT IT:

Adam and Eve had everything they could have ever wanted, but they gave into temptation. What could Adam and Eve have done differently? What would you do if you were tempted with something you know isn't right?

Memory Verse:
"So God created human beings in his own image. In the image of God, he created them; male and female he created them." Genesis 1:27
To learn more about Adam & Eve , read Genesis 1-3

CAIN & ABEL

Cain and Abel were the first two sons of Adam and Eve. Cain was a farmer who offered fruits from his land, while Abel was a shepherd who brought the best lamb from his flock. God was pleased with Abel's gift but did not accept Cain's, which made Cain very upset and jealous. Instead of talking to God about his feelings, Cain let his anger take over and ended up hurting Abel. This story teaches us the importance of being kind to one another and how we should handle our emotions in a way that pleases God.

THINK ABOUT IT:
Cain let his jealousy and anger get the best of him, leading to a big mistake. Can you think of a time when you felt jealous or angry? What helped you calm down and make a better choice?

Memory Verse:
"Don't let evil conquer you, but conquer evil by doing good."
Romans 12:21
To learn more about Cain and Abel, read Matthew 14 and John 21

NOAH

Noah was a man who loved and obeyed God, even when no one else did. One day, God told Noah to build a huge ark to save his family and the animals from a great flood. Noah trusted God and built the ark, bringing two of every animal inside. After 40 days of rain, the waters covered the earth, but Noah, his family, and the animals were safe. When the flood ended, God placed a rainbow in the sky as a promise to never flood the earth again. This story teaches us to have faith and follow God's commands, even if we don't fully understand.

THINK ABOUT IT:

Noah did what he was instructed, even when people didn't understand. Do you think it is hard to obey the rules, even when your friends don't? What would you do if you were in a similar situation?

Memory Verse:
"Noah was a righteous man, the only blameless person living on earth at the time, and he walked in close fellowship with God."
Genesis 6:9
To read more about Noah's story, read Genesis 5-10

ABRAHAM

Abraham was a man who trusted God, even when things seemed impossible. God promised Abraham that he would have a big family, as many as the stars in the sky, even though he and his wife Sarah were very old. One day, God gave them a son named Isaac, fulfilling His promise. Because of Abraham's faith, God blessed him and made him the father of many nations! This story teaches us the importance of trusting in God's plan, even when it seems impossible.

Think About It:

Abraham had to put his full trust in God, even though he didn't see how it would be possible. Do you fully trust God with every area of your life? What is something that seems impossible but with God it can actually happen?

Memory Verse:

"And Abraham believed the Lord, and the Lord counted him as righteous because of his faith." Genesis 15:6

To read more about Noah's story, read Genesis 12-25

SARAH

Sarah was a woman who waited a very long time for a special promise from God. Even though she was old, God promised that she and her husband, Abraham, would have a son. Sarah laughed when she first heard this because it seemed impossible! But God kept His promise, and soon they had a baby boy named Isaac. Sarah's story teaches us that nothing is too hard for God and that we can trust His promises, even if they take time.

THINK ABOUT IT:

Sarah had to wait a long time for God's promise. Can you think of a time when you had to wait for something you really wanted? How did it feel when it finally happened?

Memory Verse:

"Let us hold tightly without wavering to the hope we affirm,for God can be trusted to keep His promise." Hebrews 10:23

To read more about Sarah's story, read Genesis 16-18

JOSEPH

Joseph was one of twelve brothers. His father, Jacob, loved him very much and gave him a special colorful coat. His brothers were jealous and sold him into slavery, but Joseph trusted God through every hardship. In Egypt, he became an important leader, and when a famine struck, Joseph's brothers came to Egypt for help. Instead of being angry, Joseph showed kindness and forgave them. Joseph's story reminds us that forgiveness is powerful.

THINK ABOUT IT:

Joseph chose to forgive his brothers, even though they had hurt him. Can you think of a time when someone hurt your feelings? How did it feel to forgive them, or how would it feel if you did?

Memory Verse:
"You intended to harm me, but God intended it all for good. He brought me to this position so I could save the lives of many people." Genesis 50:20

To read more about Joseph's story, read Genesis 37-50

MOSES

When Moses was born, Pharaoh wanted to harm all Hebrew baby boys. His mother hid him in a basket in the river to keep him safe. Pharaoh's daughter found him and raised Moses in the palace. When he was older, God called Moses to lead the Israelites out of Egypt and free them from slavery. With God's help, Moses parted the Red Sea so the people could escape, and they traveled toward the promised land. Moses' story shows us that God can use us in amazing ways when we trust and follow Him.

THINK ABOUT IT:
Moses faced a lot of challenges, but he trusted God to help him. Can you think of a time when you had to be brave to do something difficult? How did trusting someone or something help you through it?

Memory Verse:
"The Lord himself will fight for you. Just stay calm."
Exodus 14:14
To read more about Moses' story, read Exodus 3-14

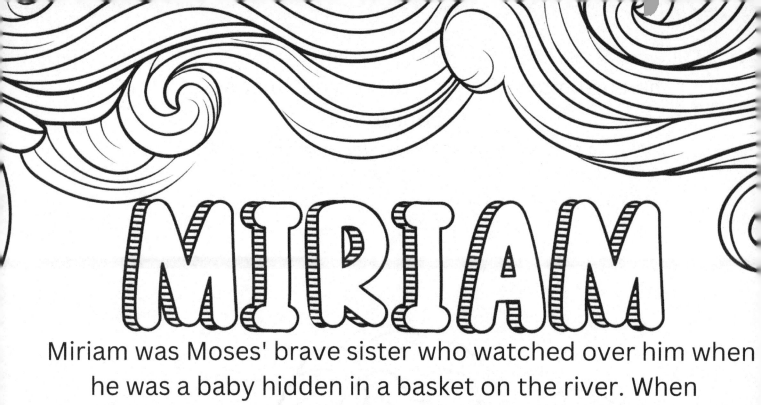

MIRIAM

Miriam was Moses' brave sister who watched over him when he was a baby hidden in a basket on the river. When Pharaoh's daughter found Moses, Miriam offered to find a nurse for him—bringing him back to their own mother for a time! Years later, after God helped Moses lead the Israelites out of Egypt, Miriam led the people in singing and dancing to thank God. She became a leader among her people and trusted God through many challenges. Miriam's story reminds us of the power of courage, kindness, and praising God in all things.

THINK ABOUT IT:

Miriam showed courage and kindness by helping her brother and praising God during difficult times. Can you think of a time when you helped someone or showed kindness, even when it was hard?
How did it make you feel?

Memory Verse:
"Let everything that breathes sings praises to the Lord!"
Psalm 150:6
To read more about Miriam's story, read Exodus 2:1-10

JOSHUA

Joshua was a faithful helper to Moses and a brave leader chosen by God to lead the Israelites into the Promised Land. When they came to the city of Jericho, God told Joshua to have the people march around the city walls for seven days. On the seventh day, they marched around seven times, blew their trumpets, and shouted—and the walls of Jericho came tumbling down! Joshua trusted God's plan, even when it seemed unusual, and God gave them victory. Joshua's story teaches us that with faith and obedience, God can help us overcome any challenge.

THINK ABOUT IT:
Joshua trusted God's plan, even when it seemed strange. Can you think of a time when something seemed unusual or hard to understand, but you trusted it anyway? What happened?

Memory Verse:
"This is my command- be strong and courageous! Do not be afraid or discouraged. For the Lord your God is with you wherever you go." Joshua 1:9

To read more about Joshua's story, read Joshua 1-6

DEBORAH

Deborah was a wise leader and judge in Israel, and people came to her for guidance and help. One day, God told Deborah to lead Israel into battle against a powerful army, and she called a brave warrior named Barak to help. Barak asked Deborah to go with him, and together, they trusted God and defeated their enemies. After the victory, Deborah sang a song to praise God for His help. Deborah's story shows us that God can use anyone—boys and girls, men and women—to do great things when we follow Him.

THINK ABOUT IT:

Deborah showed courage and trusted God to do something that seemed impossible. Can you think of a time when you needed to be brave to do the right thing? How did it turn out?

Memory Verse:
"God is our refuge and strength, always ready to help in times of trouble." Psalm 46:1

To read more about Deborah's story, read Judges 4-5

GIDEON

Gideon was a man who felt small and weak, but God called him to lead the Israelites against their enemies, the Midianites. Even though Gideon was unsure, he trusted God and gathered an army. God told Gideon to make his army smaller—only 300 men—so everyone would see that God gave them the victory. Using only torches, trumpets, and jars, Gideon's small army scared the Midianites and won the battle without even fighting. Gideon's story reminds us that with God's strength, we can do big things, no matter how small we feel.

THINK ABOUT IT:

Gideon felt small and unsure, but he trusted God and did something great. Can you think of a time when you felt too small or not strong enough to do something? What happened when you tried anyway?

Memory Verse:
"The angel of the Lord appeared to him and said,
'Mighty hero, the Lord is with you.'" Judges 6:12
To read more about Gideon's story, read Judges 6-7

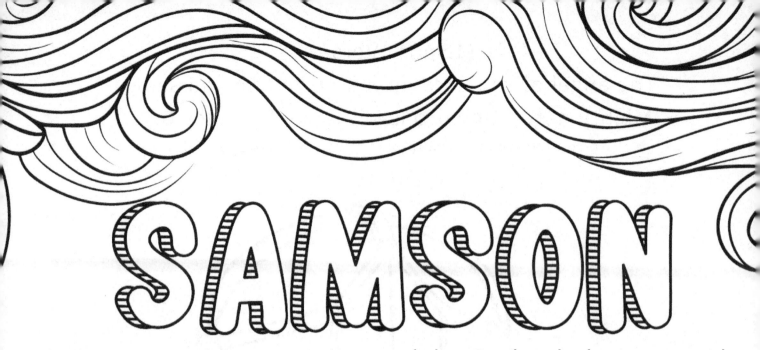

SAMSON

Samson was given great strength by God to help protect the Israelites from their enemies, the Philistines. He made a special promise to God and never cut his hair, which was a sign of his strength. But Samson made some unwise choices, and his enemies tricked him into revealing that his strength came from his uncut hair. They cut his hair, causing him to lose his strength. Samson prayed to God for one last chance to help his people. God answered, and Samson pushed down the pillars of a Philistine temple, showing that God is always ready to forgive and help us when we turn back to Him.

THINK ABOUT IT:
Samson made mistakes but prayed to God for a second chance, and God helped him. Can you think of a time when you made a mistake and needed a second chance? How did it feel to be forgiven or to try again?

Memory Verse:
"But if we confess our sins to him, He is faithful and just to forgive us of our sins and to cleanse us from all wickedness."
1 John 1:9
To read more about Samson's story, read Judges 13-16

RUTH

Ruth was a kind woman from Moab who chose to stay with her mother-in-law, Naomi, after they both lost their husbands. Even though Ruth could have gone back to her own family, she told Naomi, "Your people will be my people, and your God will be my God." Ruth worked hard to take care of Naomi and gathered grain in the fields. God blessed Ruth for her kindness, and she later married Boaz, a kind man who provided for them. Ruth's story reminds us of loyalty, love, and how God cares for those who trust Him and care for others.

THINK ABOUT IT:

Ruth chose to stay with Naomi, showing love and loyalty, even when it was hard. Can you think of a time when you chose to help someone or stick by a friend, even when it wasn't easy? How did it make you feel to do the right thing?

Memory Verse:
"Never let loyalty and kindness leave you! Tie them around your neck as a reminder. Write them deep within your heart."
Proverbs 3:3
To read more about Ruth's story, read the book of Ruth

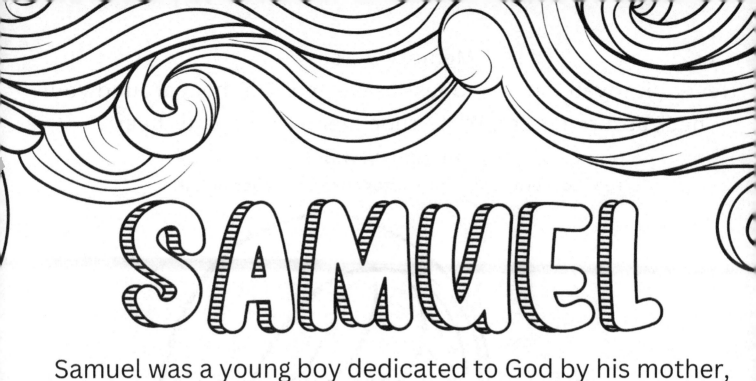

SAMUEL

Samuel was a young boy dedicated to God by his mother, Hannah, and he lived and served in the temple with the priest Eli. One night, Samuel heard a voice calling his name and thought it was Eli, but it was actually God speaking to him! Eli told Samuel to listen, so when God called again, Samuel answered, "Speak, Lord, for your servant is listening." As Samuel grew, God used him as a prophet to help lead and guide the Israelites. Samuel's story shows us the importance of listening to God and being ready to follow His words.

THINK ABOUT IT:

Samuel listened when God called him, even when he didn't understand at first. Can you think of a time when you had to listen carefully to someone important, like a parent or a teacher? How did listening help you do the right thing?

Memory Verse:
"I listen carefully to what God the Lord is saying, for he speaks peace to his faithful people." Psalm 85:8
To read more about Samuel's story, read the book of 1 Samuel

DAVID

David was a young shepherd who loved God and trusted Him with all his heart. When a giant named Goliath threatened the Israelites, David bravely stepped forward with just a sling and five stones. With God's help, David defeated Goliath, showing everyone that no one is too small when God is on their side. Later, David became a king known for his love for God and for writing many of the Psalms. David's story teaches us that God can use us in big ways when we trust Him and have courage.

THINK ABOUT IT:

David faced a giant with courage because he trusted God. Can you think of a time when you had to face something that seemed too big or scary? What helped you be brave?

Memory Verse:
"David said to the Philistine, 'You come against me with sword, spear and javelin, but I come against you in the name of the Lord Almighty.'" 1 Samuel 17:45

To read more about David's story, read the books of 1 and 2 Samuel

SOLOMON

Solomon was the son of King David and became the king of Israel known for his great wisdom. One day, God asked Solomon what he wanted, and instead of asking for riches or a long life, Solomon asked for wisdom to lead his people well. God was pleased with Solomon's request and gave him not only wisdom but also wealth and honor. Solomon built a magnificent temple for God, where the people could worship Him. His story reminds us that asking God for wisdom is one of the best things we can do to help others and make good choices.

THINK ABOUT IT:
Solomon could have asked for anything but chose to ask God for wisdom. If you could ask God for one thing to help you or others, what would it be? Why?

Memory Verse:
"If you need wisdom, ask our generous God, and he will give it to you. He will not rebuke you for asking." James 1:5
To read more about Solomon's story, read 1 Kings 1-11, 2 Chronicles 1-9, and 2 Samuel 10-12

ELIJAH

Elijah was a prophet who loved and served God during a time when many people had turned away from Him. One day, he challenged the prophets of the false god Baal to a contest on Mount Carmel to show who was the true God. Elijah built an altar and called on God to send fire from heaven, and God answered by sending fire to consume the sacrifice, proving He was the one true God! After this great victory, Elijah ran away to a cave because he was scared of Queen Jezebel, but God spoke to him in a gentle whisper, reminding him that he was not alone. Elijah's story teaches us that God is always with us, and He can give us strength when we face challenges.

THINK ABOUT IT:

Elijah was brave, but even he felt scared sometimes. Can you think of a time when you felt afraid or alone? How did you find comfort, or who helped you feel better?

Memory Verse:
"Don't be afraid, for I am with you. Don't be discouraged, for I am your God. I will strengthen you and help you. I will hold you up with my victorious right hand." Isaiah 41:10

To read more about Elijah's story, read 1 Kings 17-19 and 2 Kings 1-2

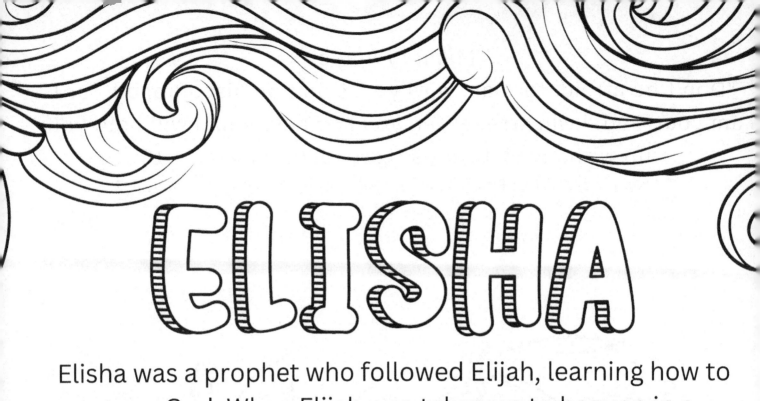

ELISHA

Elisha was a prophet who followed Elijah, learning how to serve God. When Elijah was taken up to heaven in a whirlwind, Elisha received a double portion of Elijah's spirit and continued to share God's message with the people. One day, Elisha performed a miracle by making a pot of poisonous stew safe to eat, showing God's power to protect His people. He also helped a widow by providing her with enough oil to pay her debts and keep her family safe. Elisha's story reminds us that God can do amazing things through us when we trust and obey Him.

THINK ABOUT IT:

Elisha helped others by trusting God and using the gifts God gave him. Can you think of a time when you helped someone in need? How did it feel to make a difference in their life?

Memory Verse:
"Trust in the Lord with all your heart; do not depend on your own understanding." Proverbs 3:5

To read more about Elisha's story, read 2 Kings 2-5

ESTHER

Esther was a brave young Jewish woman who became the queen of Persia while keeping her identity a secret. When a wicked man named Haman plotted to harm her people, Esther's cousin Mordecai urged her to speak up and save them. Esther was afraid, but she trusted God and decided to approach the king, risking her life to reveal her true identity. She invited the king and Haman to a special dinner, where she courageously exposed Haman's evil plan. Because of Esther's bravery, the king stopped Haman, and her people were saved. This story teaches us that we can make a difference when we stand up for what is right.

THINK ABOUT IT:

Esther was afraid but still spoke up to protect her people. Can you think of a time when you had to be brave to stand up for what was right, even if it was hard? What happened?

Memory Verse:
"This is my command- be strong and courageous! Do not be afraid or discouraged. For the Lord your God is with you wherever you go." Joshua 1:9
To read more about Esther's story, read the book of Esther

DANIEL

Daniel was a young man taken to Babylon, where he served King Nebuchadnezzar and showed great wisdom and faith in God. When the king made a rule that no one could pray to anyone except him, Daniel continued to pray to God three times a day, knowing it was the right thing to do. As a result, he was thrown into a den of hungry lions, but God sent an angel to protect him, and the lions did not harm him! The next morning, the king was amazed to find Daniel safe and unharmed. Daniel's story teaches us the importance of staying true to our faith and trusting God, even in difficult situations.

THINK ABOUT IT:

Daniel chose to pray to God even when it was dangerous. Can you think of a time when you stood up for what you believed was right, even if others didn't agree? How did it make you feel afterward?

Memory Verse:

"But when I am afraid, I will be put my trust in you." Psalm 56:3

To read more about Daniel's story, read the book of Daniel

SHADRACH, MESHACH AND ABEDNEGO

Shadrach, Meshach, and Abednego were three friends who loved and served God while living in Babylon. When King Nebuchadnezzar made a giant gold statue and ordered everyone to bow down to it, these three friends refused because they knew it was wrong to worship anyone but God. The king was furious and threw them into a fiery furnace. They bravely said that God could save them if He chose to do so. He did indeed- He sent an angel to protect them, and they walked around unharmed in the flames! The king was amazed and recognized the power of their God. When we stand up for what is right, God is always with us.

THINK ABOUT IT:

They stood up for what they believed, even when it was very scary. Can you think of a time when you had to be brave to do the right thing? How did it feel to stay true to what you believed?

Memory Verse:
"The Lord is my helper, so I will have no fear. What can mere people do to me?" Hebrews 13:6
To read more about Shadrach, Meshach, and Abednego's story, read Daniel 3

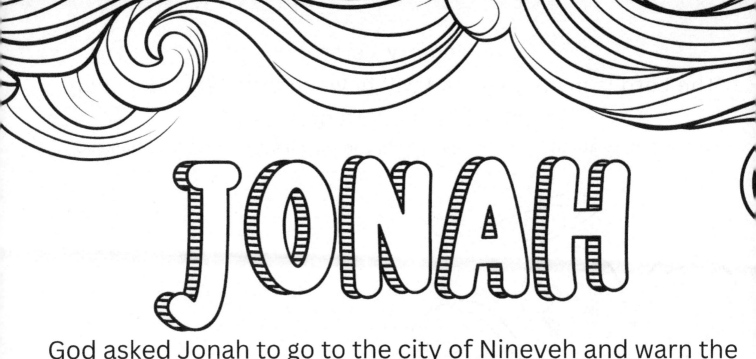

JONAH

God asked Jonah to go to the city of Nineveh and warn the people to turn away from their bad ways. Jonah didn't want to go, so he ran away on a ship. A great storm arose, and Jonah told the sailors it was his fault, so they threw Jonah overboard to calm the sea. God sent a big fish to swallow Jonah, and he spent three days and three nights in its belly, praying and asking for forgiveness. When the fish spit Jonah out onto dry land he obeyed God and went to Nineveh. The people of Nineveh listened, repented, and turned back to God, teaching us that it's never too late to listen to God and do what is right.

THINK ABOUT IT:

Jonah ran away from God, but was given a second chance to make things right. Can you think of a time when you tried to avoid doing something difficult but decided to do it anyway? How did it feel when you finally did the right thing?

Memory Verse:
"'So let us come boldly to the throne of our gracious God. There we will receive his mercy, and we will find grace to help us when we need it most." Hebrews 4:16

To read more about Jonah's story, read the book of Jonah

JESUS

Jesus was born in Bethlehem to Mary and Joseph, and His birth was announced by angels as a special gift from God. As He grew up, Jesus performed many miracles, such as healing the sick, calming storms, and even bringing people back to life, showing God's love and power. He taught people about God's kingdom, sharing stories called parables that helped them understand how to love one another. Jesus showed the greatest love of all by dying on the cross for our sins and then rising again three days later. His story teaches us about God's amazing love, forgiveness, and the promise of eternal life for everyone who believes in Him.

THINK ABOUT IT:

Jesus showed the greatest love by giving His life for others. Can you think of a time when someone showed you kindness or love that made you feel special? How can you show that same kind of love to others?

Memory Verse:
"For this is how God loved the world, He gave us his one and only Son, so that everyone who believes in him will not perish but have eternal life." John 3:16

To read more about Jesus' story, read the gospels- Matthew, Mark, Luke, & John

JOHN THE BAPTIST

John the Baptist was a special messenger from God who came to prepare the way for Jesus. He lived in the wilderness and wore rough clothes made of camel's hair and ate locusts and wild honey. John preached to the people, telling them to turn away from their sins and be baptized to show they wanted to follow God. One day, he saw Jesus coming and exclaimed that Jesus was the Lamb of God who takes away the sins of the world! John baptized Jesus in the Jordan River, and God showed everyone that Jesus was His beloved Son, teaching us the importance of following God's plan and sharing His message.

THINK ABOUT IT:

John spent his days teaching the people about Jesus. Have you ever had the courage to speak the truth when it was hard? How do you think you could be a messenger for God?

Memory Verse:
"He must become greater and greater, and I must become less and less." John 3:30
To read more about John the Baptist's story, read Matthew 3

MARY

Mary was a young woman living in Nazareth when an angel named Gabriel visited her with an amazing message: she would be the mother of God's son, Jesus! At first, Mary was surprised and confused, but she trusted God. When it was time for Jesus to be born, Mary and Joseph traveled to Bethlehem, where Jesus was born in a stable because there was no room for them in the inn. Mary cared for Jesus as He grew, and she treasured all the special moments in her heart. Mary's story teaches us about faith, obedience, and the incredible love of a mother.

THINK ABOUT IT:

Mary trusted God even when she didn't understand everything that was happening. Can you think of a time when you had to trust someone, even if you were unsure or afraid? How did it turn out?

Memory Verse:
"Mary responded, 'I am the Lords servant. May everything you have said about me come true.' and then the angel left her."
Luke 1:38
To read more about Mary's story, read Luke 1

THE GOOD SAMARITAN

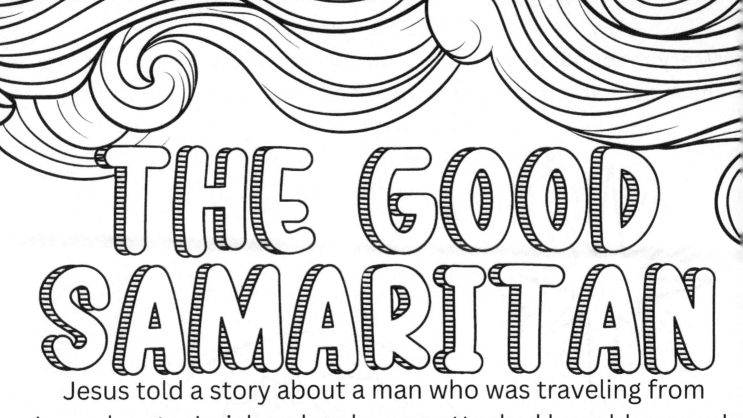

Jesus told a story about a man who was traveling from Jerusalem to Jericho when he was attacked by robbers and left hurt by the side of the road. Many people passed by him, including a priest and a Levite, but they did not stop to help. Then a Samaritan, who was from a group that the Jews didn't usually like, saw the man and felt compassion for him. The Samaritan bandaged the man's wounds, took him to an inn, and paid for his care. Jesus used this story to teach us that we should love and help everyone, no matter who they are, just like the Good Samaritan did.

THINK ABOUT IT:

Jesus taught that we should help others, even if they are different from us. Can you think of a time when you helped someone in need, or when someone helped you? How did that act of kindness make you feel?

Memory Verse:

"Love your neighbor as yourself." Mark 12:31

To read more about The Good Samaritan's story, read Luke 10:25-37

MARTHA

Martha was a kind and caring woman who loved Jesus and welcomed Him into her home. One day, while Jesus was visiting, Martha was busy preparing a big meal, while her sister Mary sat at Jesus' feet, listening to Him teach. Martha felt overwhelmed and asked Jesus to tell Mary to help her, but Jesus gently reminded her that spending time with Him was the most important thing. He encouraged Martha to find peace in listening and learning instead of just working. Martha's story teaches us that while it's good to help and serve, we should also take time to be with Jesus and learn from Him.

THINK ABOUT IT:
Martha was busy, but Jesus reminded her to take time to listen. Can you think of a time when you were so busy with something that you missed out on spending time with someone? How did it feel to stop and just be with them?

Memory Verse:
"Come close to God, and God will come close to you. Wash your hands, you sinners; purify your hearts, for your loyalty is divided between God and the world." James 4:8
To read more about Martha's story, read Luke 10:38-42

ZACCHAEUS

Zacchaeus was a wealthy tax collector in Jericho, but the people did not like him because he took more money than he should have. One day, when Jesus was passing through the town, Zacchaeus wanted to see Him but was too short to see over the crowd. So, he climbed up a sycamore tree to get a better view. To his surprise, Jesus stopped right under the tree and called him by name, saying He would stay at Zacchaeus's house that day. Zacchaeus was so happy that he changed his ways and promised to give half of his wealth to the poor and repay anyone he had cheated. This story teaches us that it's never too late to turn to Jesus and make things right.

THINK ABOUT IT:

Zacchaeus changed his ways after meeting Jesus and made things right with the people he had hurt. Can you think of a time when you made a mistake but tried to fix it? How did it feel to do the right thing afterward?

Memory Verse:
"For the Son of Man came to seek and save those who are lost."
Luke 19:10
To read more about Zacchaeus' story, read Luke 19:1-10

PAUL

Paul, named Saul before his conversion, was a man who initially did not believe in Jesus and tried to stop others from following Him. One day, while traveling to Damascus, a bright light from heaven blinded him, and he heard the voice of Jesus asking, "Why are you persecuting me?" After this powerful encounter, Paul became a follower of Jesus and was healed of his blindness. He traveled far and wide, sharing the good news about Jesus and helping many people learn about God's love. Paul's story teaches us that God can change our hearts and use us for great things, no matter what our past looks like.

THINK ABOUT IT:

Paul's heart was changed after he met Jesus, and he spent the rest of his life helping others know God. Can you think of a time when you changed your mind about something? What made you decide to change, and how did it feel afterward?

Memory Verse:
"This means that anyone who belongs to Christ has become a new person. The old life is gone; a new life has begun."
2 Corinthians 5:17
To read more about Paul's story, read Acts 9

SILAS

Silas was a faithful friend and helper of the Apostle Paul, traveling with him to spread the message of Jesus. One day, while they were in the city of Philippi, they were arrested for doing God's work. Even in prison, instead of feeling afraid, Silas and Paul sang songs and prayed to God at midnight. Suddenly, there was a powerful earthquake that shook the prison, opening the doors. But they didn't leave! The jailer was so amazed that he asked how he could be saved, and Silas and Paul shared the good news about Jesus with him, showing us that God is always with us, even in tough times.

THINK ABOUT IT:

Silas and Paul prayed and sang songs even when they were in a tough situation. Can you think of a time when you chose to stay positive or pray during a difficult time? How did it help you feel better?

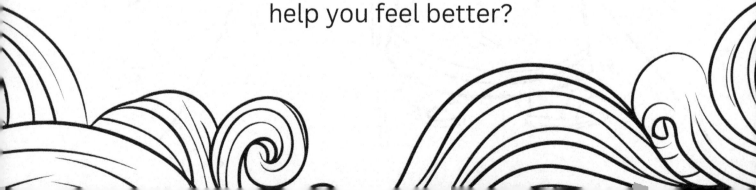

Memory Verse:
"Be thankful in all circumstances, for this is God's will for you who belong to Christ Jesus." 1 Thessalonians 5:18

To read more about Silas' story, read Acts 16:25-31

Made in the USA
Coppell, TX
14 December 2024

42501609R00037